Original title:

Whispers of an Island Breeze

Copyright © 2025 Creative Arts Management OÜ
All rights reserved.

Author: Samuel Kensington
ISBN HARDBACK: 978-1-80581-505-1
ISBN PAPERBACK: 978-1-80581-032-2
ISBN EBOOK: 978-1-80581-505-1

The Song of a Traveler's Heart

A suitcase filled with mismatched socks,
A map that shows the wrong old docks,
With laughter ringing through the air,
I trip on flip-flops without a care.

The sun is hot, my drink is cold,
I dance like I'm a bit too bold,
The waves invite me for a spin,
While seagulls laugh at this old grin.

Caressing Wind on Weathered Faces

A gust of air, it steals my hat,
A sneaky bird, it knows just that,
With beach balls flying, I stand tall,
And trip over a tiny shellball.

The breeze, it giggles like a friend,
With salty kisses that never end,
My hair's a mess, but that's just fine,
For laughter flows like summer wine.

Dreams Floating on the Ocean's Breath

With dreams adrift on waves so blue,
I try to surf, but fall, it's true,
A dolphin laughs, he's in on the joke,
As I splash down like an old oak.

The sun begins to set its stage,
While I play tag with a cheeky sage,
A crab strolls by with a dance in its gait,
Stealing my snack while I contemplate.

The Language of Seaglass and Breeze

The ocean speaks in bits of glass,
With secrets that come and go like grass,
I gather treasures, sharp yet bright,
A pirate's hoard, just out of sight.

The breeze composes a silly song,
While I conduct, my limbs go wrong,
With each wave, a graceful twist,
But tripping over winds is hard to resist.

Reflections on the Surface of Dreams

In the land where palm trees sway,
The birds argue who will play.
A crab tries dancing, in a line,
While seagulls giggle, drinking brine.

Turtles race, but just for fun,
In a wobbly shell, they run.
But when the sun begins to set,
They forget who won, and that's a debt.

The fish tell tales of lovers lost,
While seaweed sways, it's not the cost.
A dolphin jumps, thinks he's a star,
But lands right next to a clam bazaar.

With each wave, a laugh rings out,
A sand crab sings, without a doubt.
In dreams of surf and playful light,
The memory of joy takes flight.

Enchanted Breezes in the Afternoon Light

The breeze tickles the cheeky sand,
As flip-flops fly from foot to hand.
Seashells giggle, their secrets shared,
While ocean jokes are cleverly aired.

A starfish dressed in flashy wear,
Himself, he twirls with utmost flair.
A wave slides in, to steal the scene,
While barnacles sigh, 'That's quite obscene!'

A gentle breeze wraps 'round the dunes,
While crabs debate to whistle tunes.
The sun melts down, the laughter glows,
As riptides dance and moonlight flows.

With sandy feet and salty dreams,
The daytime ends in giggling schemes.
In every gust, a story formed,
As the evening's antics keep us warmed.

The Breath of Distant Shores

Seagulls squawk at the beach so bright,
While tourists slip in sunscreen fight.
Crabs dance sideways with silly flair,
As sandcastles lean, unaware of their scare.

A beach ball flies, a rogue in the sun,
Dodging kids, oh what a run!
Shells scatter like lost thoughts in the sand,
And laughter echoes across the land.

Murmurs Beneath Tropical Canopies

Coconuts drop like clumsy dreams,
While monkeys plot with leafy schemes.
Bananas smile, stuck in a bunch,
Giggling quietly, never a punch.

Lizards stare with a judging glance,
As tourists try their clumsy dance.
The vines sway, teasing the heat,
While chattering parrots repeat 'Repeat!'

Songs of the Swaying Palms

Palms sway gently, a funky tune,
Dancers twirl beneath a bouncy moon.
Bikini tops fly in the warm breeze,
While flip-flops dance with buzzing bees.

Cocktails clink, a fruity cheer,
Tipping umbrellas—oh dear, oh dear!
Mischief fills the tropical air,
As laughter bounces everywhere.

Eddies of Nighttime Tumult

The waves crash loud in a bubbly jest,
As the night creeps in, ruffled and dressed.
Fireflies blink like cheeky sprites,
While frogs croak out their starry nights.

Cool breezes tease and play hide and seek,
With every rustle, there's laughter to speak.
Ghost crabs scuttle with comical flair,
As the moon shares secrets with sandy air.

Lullabies of an Endless Horizon

A crab in a tux, quite the sight,
Dancing under the moon so bright.
Seagulls snicker, flying high,
As fish in the sea give a fishy goodbye.

The sandcastles lean, they sway and fall,
Kings and queens made of sand, after all.
A clam with a crown, declaring it's king,
While the ocean waves laugh at everything.

Rhythms of the Rolling Tides

The tide rolls in with a giggle and splash,
Washing over the rocks in a playful dash.
Starfish play tag on the ocean floor,
While jellyfish join in, to dance and explore.

The waves joke gently, they tease the shore,
Telling tales of pirates and treasure galore.
Salty sea dogs bark at the gulls on the fly,
All while the sun winks from the sky.

Petals that Drift on Laughing Winds

Leaves twirl around in a comical spin,
As breezes decide where the fun will begin.
Dandelions chuckle, with wishes to blow,
While the trees shake their branches in a show.

Butterflies flutter, all dressed in flair,
Landing on noses without a care.
The flowers all gossip, they gossip away,
About bees' latest buzz on a sunny day.

Tides that Speak the Language of Stars

The night sky twinkles, full of delight,
As crickets serenade the moonlit night.
Stars wink back, with a wink and a grin,
While fish gossip softly, their tales begin.

The sea whispers jokes to the sandy shore,
Even the shells want to hear more.
Laughter erupts from the depths unseen,
As the cosmos joins in on the silly scene.

Breezes that Dance with Time

The wind wore socks and twirled a hat,
Chasing after a laughing cat.
It flipped the pages of a book,
Said, "You're late for tea! Come take a look!"

A dandelion puffed with self-appeal,
Tickled the nose of a passing seal.
With every giggle, a cloud would dive,
"Come on, let's jive! Let's come alive!"

Chasing Shadows in a Sunlit Glade

In a glade where shadows dance,
A squirrel fell over in a trance.
Chasing its tail, it spun around,
While the sun winked without a sound.

The daisies giggled, the grass did sway,
As butterflies had a grand ballet.
A rabbit tripped, slipped on a twig,
And the whole glade burst into a jig!

Currents of Dreams on High

Balloons floated up, bright and bold,
Telling secrets the stars had told.
They whispered, "Skydiving's quite absurd!
Let's launch a flock of silly birds!"

Amongst the clouds, a kite took flight,
Tangled in laughter, a true delight.
While below, the fish in a pond did sing,
"Let's dance like we're the next big thing!"

Caresses from a Forgotten Shore

The waves sent jokes that splashed and teased,
With sandcastles that hummed and sneezed.
Seashells rolled over, claiming to see,
That crabs do the cha-cha, wild and free.

A pirate's hat flew onto a bird,
It squawked, "Arrr! I love a good word!"
The sun set down, slightly askew,
Whistling tunes to the ocean blue!

A Breeze

The wind tickled my hair,
It danced around my nose,
It nudged my drink in laughter,
And caused my hat to doze.

The seagulls started to squawk,
As if they'd heard a joke,
While I just sat there laughing,
And nearly choked on smoke.

A Prayer

Oh breeze, don't be too bold,
Keep sand out of my drink,
Spare me the hairball frenzy,
And let my thoughts not sink.

As I raise my eyes to skies,
I pray for calm and cheer,
May all my worries giggle,
And just disappear from here.

A Memory

I recall the beachside games,
With friends who loved to tease,
The wind would blow our kites high,
And sweep away our knees.

Belly laughs and sandy toes,
With every gust a thrill,
Each breeze brought back a memory,
Of joy I can't quite fill.

Fragments of Light Along the Shoreline

Underneath the sparkling sun,
We chased the glimmers bright,
The breeze would play its tricks on us,
Turning day into night.

With squishy feet in salty mud,
We giggled with delight,
For every wave that knocked us down,
Made getting up feel right.

Notes of Nostalgia in Fresh Air

A tune floats on the currents,
It's catchy and quite sweet,
The breeze sings silly verses,
While we shuffle our bare feet.

Each note is like a tickle,
That makes you grin and sway,
The fresh air brings back laughter,
As we toss our cares away.

Luminescent Whispers of the Night

When the sun dips low and shy,
And stars begin to peek,
The breezy chuckles linger on,
In a game of hide-and-sneak.

With fireflies as our lanterns,
We giggle through the dark,
Each breeze brings forth a secret,
That makes us laugh and hark.

The Twilight Breath of Nature

A coconut fell with a thud,
Sending seagulls into a spud.
Crabs danced a jig on the shore,
While the shells rolled like a chore.

Stars joined in, winking their light,
As the beach became a delight.
The ocean chuckled, waves grinned wide,
In this playful nature-based ride.

Palms swayed, held their hats on tight,
Dodging the breeze in sheer delight.
Fish flipped jokes to the sandy floor,
As laughter mingled with salty shore.

Moonbeams sneaked an evening peek,
As turtles grooved, not being meek.
Nature giggled, raucous and bold,
Telling secrets as the night rolled cold.

Echoes Through Boughs of Palm

A parrot squawked in a high-pitched tune,
While crabs pranced under the lazy moon.
The palms clapped their hands, oh so spry,
Echoes of giggles float up to the sky.

The fish below were in grand dispute,
Debating who had the brightest boot.
They flapped their fins in a fishy brag,
Underwater antics made everyone sag.

Oh, the sand was soft, a clubhouse spree,
With sandcastles built for the crabby VIP.
Sea turtles cheered, waving their fins,
In this wacky world, the laughter begins.

Palm leaves rustled, telling tales,
Of cheeky dolphins and their scales.
The breeze giggled, a ticklish tease,
As nature's party swayed with ease.

Tides of Silence and Serenity

The turtles raced with zeal and might,
Competing to reach the shoreline light.
Each splash a beacon, bold and loud,
While the crabs cheered from their sandy crowd.

A gull swooped down, looking for snacks,
As fish tried to hide from its crafty tracks.
With flops and flips, on their tails they spun,
In this fishy race, who would be done?

Seashells laughed, telling secrets of old,
As the tide pulled in, both shy and bold.
The breeze nudged waves, playing pranks delight,
Turning calm shores into a silly fight.

Seagulls chirped gossip in a fast-paced spree,
While the ocean hummed a soft melody.
Under the moon, the night danced with glee,
In this tidal tale of humor and spree.

Unseen Currents of Affection

An octopus painted in colors bright,
Waved to a starfish who danced with light.
They twirled and spun without a care,
While the seaweed wiggled, adding flair.

Dolphins played a game of tag,
Their laughter echoing, no one could brag.
The ocean floor was a stage of fun,
Where jellyfish joined in, all on the run.

A clam shut tight, trying to hide,
As a cheeky crab snuck in for the ride.
They rolled with joy, in mismatched attire,
In this underwater party, never to tire.

The tide blew a kiss to the moon up high,
As the stars winked their approval to the sky.
Together they all shared a whimsical dream,
Swaying with laughter in the ocean's beam.

The Laughter of Rolling Waves

The waves tell jokes, they crash and roll,
While crabs do the cha-cha, playing their role.
Seagulls cackle, a feathered crew,
Trying to steal snacks, oh, silly they do.

The sun beams down, a spotlight on sand,
Kids building castles with a goofy hand.
A flip-flop flies, a toe takes flight,
Watch out, my chair! It's a comedic sight.

Dolphins dance, they show off their flair,
Plunging and diving like they just don't care.
A splash of water, a squeal from a child,
Wet and wild laughter, beach days are styled.

So come on down, bring your best grin,
Let the rolling waves pull you right in.
With sandy toes and smiles to chase,
Each moment a giggle, a sunny embrace.

Serene Echoes from Salted Air

The sea breeze chuckles, with secrets to tell,
It tousles our hair, and we giggle so well.
A pair of flip-flops race across the shore,
One takes a leap, shouting 'I want more!'

Salted air tickles, makes noses all twitch,
Seagull on watch, like a feathered rich.
It swoops by quick, a snack in its beak,
While everyone shouts, 'Hey, that's not a peek!'

Tide pools are stages for crabs to perform,
With pincers raised high, they break from the norm.
An audience gathers, with laughter a-bloom,
As one little crab tries to dance in a room.

So let the breezes embrace us with cheer,
On this silly island, there's nothing to fear.
With giggles and splashes, let's clink our glass,
To the joyful symphony, as moments just pass.

Breeze Kisses the Golden Sands

An ocean zephyr dances, tickling our toes,
Sandy surprises where nobody knows.
A group of sunbathers, snug in their spots,
Try to relax, but they're tangled in knots.

A beach ball soars, like a bird on the run,
It bops on a head and lands with a thud, fun!
Laughter erupts, and we cheer for the ball,
No one is safe in this comical sprawl.

Kites fight the wind, they twist with delight,
Pulling their owners to dizzy heights.
But oh! What a tumble, they whirl and they trip,
A flap of the fabric turns into a skip.

So here we gather, let the giggles expand,
With the funny little antics that smoothen our plans.
A perfect day out, with laughter to share,
As breezes come forth, tickling the air.

Tales from the Horizon's Embrace

The horizon winks, as the sun starts to play,
With colors like jellybeans, brightening the way.
Sandy toes wiggle, squeaking in glee,
As surfboards bob, oh! Look at the spree!

The sea turtle grins, with a slow, funny stride,
It's in a race with a lobster, with shell open wide.
The fish cheer them on from under the waves,
While octopuses wave like they've had wages.

A sunset parade, with beachgoers all cheered,
Chairs tumble down, and ice cream disappeared.
A seagull swoops down, causing mayhem and clatter,
As beach towels flap like they might start to chatter.

So gather your friends, bring laughter anew,
With tales and saltwater, and skies so blue.
Like playful waves curling, we'll rejoice and embrace,
With every foolish moment, let joy fill the space.

Hums of Hidden Flora

In the garden, flowers sing,
They giggle when the bees take wing.
Tulips tease with their bright caps,
While daisies share the silliest of laps.

A rose tells tales of love quite grand,
But in a daisy, humor's close at hand.
Cacti chuckle at the bumblebee's plight,
As they dodge the prickles with all their might.

Reflections in the Glassy Water

Puddles bubble, mirror the sky,
Frogs leap in, oh my, oh my!
Each ripple laughs at a passing shoe,
As fish play peek-a-boo, just for you.

The ducks all waddle with a familiar strut,
Honk and quack, what a noise they utter!
They play a game of who can float best,
While turtles roll their eyes, taking a rest.

Gentle Hums of Coastal Calm

Seagulls squawk with flair and pride,
As they ride the waves, side by side.
Sandcastles rise, a noble quest,
But the tide has other plans, oh what a jest!

Children giggle, bury their friends,
While crabs plot escape through funny bends.
A beach ball flies, a wild, silly roam,
As every splash says, 'This is home!'

Secrets Carried by Sea Winds

The breeze whispers tales, oh so sly,
Of fish who leap and birds that fly.
Clams call out with their pearl-like grin,
While the lobster's dance makes everyone spin.

Shells hold secrets, if you lean in close,
But if they snag your toe, that's no fun dose!
A lighthearted gale teases the beach,
With every gust, it's laughter they reach.

Morning's Embrace on Sandy Shores

Seagulls squawk like they own the place,
Chasing shadows with silly grace.
Coffee spills on my beachy hat,
I'm the star of this morning spat!

Sandy toes in my frosty drink,
Sunbathers squint and stop to think.
Laughter dances with the morning sun,
In this sandy circus, life's all in fun.

Crabs in a conga, they strut and boast,
Start with a shuffle, then they roast.
Everyone's here to join the game,
Morning mischief, oh what a claim!

Flip-flops flying, it's quite a sight,
Dancing under the golden light.
Let's toast with shells, let worries cease,
Lucky are we, in morning's piece!

Stories of the Driftwood's Journey

Once a tree, now a world traveler bold,
Floating stories that never get old.
Adventures shared with the tides of fate,
Brought home by pirates, the driftwood's great!

Whispers of waves, and jokes untold,
They say it's a pirate but really it's gold.
With salty tales and barnacle friends,
Every bit scratched, yet the laughter never ends.

A crab told me of treasures rare,
Said he'd trade it all for less salty air.
Each piece of wood is a story profound,
From the ocean's belly, it's laughter unbound!

Ahoy there matey, raise your cup high,
For driftwood shenanigans never say die.
With every sunset, new tales ignite,
And the journey of laughter dances into the night!

The Tranquil Voice of Distant Waters

Gentle splashes that tickle my ear,
Echoing laughter, that's why I'm here.
Fish gossip about their swimming spree,
While seaweed giggles at the sandy plea.

The ocean's murmur is quite the jest,
As waves tumble by, they never rest.
Sea cucumbers plotting their slow parade,
"Keep it moving, don't let fun fade!"

Seagulls argue over who's top dive,
While jellyfish dance, a luminous jive.
Shells form a choir, all singing off-key,
In the symphony of fun, oh let it be!

Let's build a castle, let's make it grand,
With towers of laughter and sippy drink sand.
For in these waters, peace wears a grin,
And every splash calls for laughter within!

Requiem for an Evening Breeze

Evening breeze, oh what a tease,
Sweeping in like a giggling sneeze.
Tickling palms and tousling hair,
It's a playful prankster, flapping everywhere!

The sun's bowing out with a cheerful glance,
While beach towels dance their blushing dance.
Whispers of sand promise stories anew,
As flip-flops chase my toes, who knew?

Drinks in hand and a wink from the moon,
The breeze carries jokes of a silly tune.
Flickering candles share the spotlight,
In this breezy jest, we party all night!

Tomorrow brings sunshine, no need to mourn,
For the evening breeze, still carries a horn.
As laughter carries, just let it be,
Under starlit skies, wild and free!

Tender Caress of the Warm Zephyr

A tickle on the cheek at dawn,
The seagulls laugh, the night is gone.
Flip-flops dance along the sand,
As beach balloons escape our hands.

Sandy toes and salty hair,
Ice cream melts, no time to spare.
The sun's a prankster on the rise,
With winks and giggles in the skies.

Kites fly high, their tails a swirl,
A hula-hoop in twirls unfurl.
Dancing shells and kooky crabs,
Join the fun in wild jabs!

So let's toast to breezy tricks,
And wear our shades like funny hats.
With laughter floating in the air,
We'll make this breeze our happy lair.

Echoes of the Ocean's Breath

The tide rolls in, a clumsy cheer,
Splashing besties who come near.
Seaweed wigs on our heads we don,
Like mermaids pranking till the dawn.

Bubbles rise like giggles fine,
As sandcastles croon their line.
A crab in shades, all strut and pride,
Dancing sideways, who can hide?

Toss the frisbee, catch the wave,
On this beach, we misbehave.
With sunscreen smeared on every cheek,
The ocean shouts, "Hey, don't be meek!"

So here we are, a joyful crew,
Chasing laughter, skies so blue.
We'll surf the fun until it ends,
Each breeze a tickle, laughter blends.

Serenade of Shores Unseen

Over the dunes, a giggle flies,
As jellyfish wear their silly ties.
Sandy flatulence from the tide,
Makes everyone run off to hide!

A parrot yells, "It's time to eat!"
As picnic ants march with their feet.
Crackers crunch, a symphony,
As we munch, the ants agree.

Surfboards dance on foam so bright,
Each wipeout brings a comic plight.
With every fall, we shout hooray,
A carnival on a sunny day!

Laughter curls like smoke in air,
As sea birds join without a care.
With gales of joy, we twirl and spin,
In the song of sand, let chaos win!

Secrets of the Sweetly Swaying Ferns

Among the ferns, a secret game,
With playful squirrels, all the same.
Racing 'round, a leafy chase,
As nature giggles, we keep pace.

The breeze hums tunes of funny pranks,
We share our secrets, hide in ranks.
A lizard leaps, we squeal with glee,
In the tall grass, oh, can't you see?

Each rustling leaf plays its part,
Like whispers from a friendly heart.
We twirl and laugh, the sun our guide,
In this green world, let joy reside.

So take my hand, let's frolic more,
With ferns that dance upon the floor.
In nature's chuckle, we are found,
As laughter echoes all around.

Songs of the Rolling Dunes

In the sand, a crab does dance,
Wearing shades, it takes a chance.
Seagulls scream, oh what a sight,
They steal snacks, such a delight.

Turtles race with mighty flair,
But it's all just a little rare.
A beach ball pops, what a disaster,
The laughter rolls; we go faster!

Sunsets come, they twist and sway,
The colors bunch, in wild play.
Oh look, a sandcastle meets its doom,
As waves crash down with a big boom!

So gather 'round, the tales we weave,
Of salty pranks we won't believe.
Each grain hides giggles, loud and free,
Dunes dance with glee, such jubilee!

Tapestry of Shadows and Light

Beneath bright rays, shadows creep,
A squirrel sneaks, and starts to leap.
Cats stretch out, take up the shade,
Dreaming deep, but plans they made!

The sun sets low, colors collide,
A lizard skids, what a wild ride!
Mice in sneakers, racing quick,
They zigzag back, it's quite the trick!

Fishes jump, doing flips,
While otters glide on slippery trips.
Laughter echoing through the night,
Moon chuckles down, in pure delight.

So catch the fun, as shadows play,
With giggles that chase clouds away.
In every flicker, in every flight,
A cheerful scene of silly sight!

Portraits Painted by Wind and Sea

A breeze pulls hats off little heads,
While dolphins hop, leaving their beds.
Crabs on stilts perform their act,
As beachgoers watch, they react!

Seashells chatter, tales to share,
Mermaids giggle, toss their hair.
Jellyfish wear a funny crown,
Their dance makes everyone frown!

Tides ebb and flow, they never tire,
Surfboards zoom, we all aspire.
Kites twist high in daring flight,
Chasing dreams till the fall of night.

So join the fun, let laughter peal,
On painted waves, let's make a deal.
With every splash, let joy roam free,
In every portrait, wild jubilee!

Conversations Between Sea and Sky

Clouds tease waves with every glide,
The ocean laughs, a splashing ride.
Stars spill secrets, whispers slow,
As moonbeams shimmer, putting on a show.

Seabirds squawk, it's quite a cheer,
"Who ate my lunch?" a voice we hear!
The gale snickers, a playful gust,
As raindrops dance, oh what a bust!

Waves and winds, in frenzy talk,
"Did you see that?" with a squawk.
Each bubbly foam holds stories tight,
Creating fun, a pure delight.

Under stars and the blue expanse,
Nature's giggles lead the dance.
With every burble, each soft sigh,
The universe laughs, oh my, oh my!

Enchanted Flutters in the Dusk

As the crabs dance like they're in a show,
Seagulls cackle while the sun dips low.
Laughter echoes where the sand meets the bay,
Even the starfish cheer at the end of the day.

Flip-flops squeak with a comical sound,
A beach ball wobbles, it bounces around.
With coconut drinks and umbrellas in tow,
Who needs a plan? Let the merriment flow!

The sunsets swirl in colors so bright,
While jellyfish giggle in luminescent light.
A flip-flop flips, and someone takes a dive,
In this merry chaos, we truly come alive.

Cranky old turtles race just for fun,
With shells that gleam like they've eaten the sun.
Inhales of salty air, giggles in the breeze,
Dance with the tides, do as you please!

Mellow Tides of Memory's Song

Sandy feet shuffle on a path that's a maze,
Floating memories in the sun's golden rays.
The ocean hums softly, a laugh to the sky,
While dolphins practice their leaps, oh my!

Shells in pockets, all treasures of glee,
Each grain of sand keeps a secret, you see.
A beach umbrella steals the show with a twirl,
As kites take flight, giving laughter a whirl.

The tide rolls in with a friendly embrace,
Tickling our toes in a playful race.
We chase the waves with each joyous shout,
In this silly wonder, there's never a doubt.

Sunburnt noses and laughter abound,
This carefree rhythm is a gift that astounds.
With stories to share and smiles to prolong,
We find ourselves dancing, to memory's song.

Soliloquy of the Restless Waves

The waves chat loudly with a foamy grin,
Joking with shells, 'Come, let the fun begin!'
Sea turtles nod as they wade by in style,
While fish play peek-a-boo, all dressed in a smile.

Bubbles pop loud in a bubbly debate,
As crabs argue over who's fashionably late.
Seaweed sways like a comedic design,
In this wacky ocean, all seems just fine.

Flip-flops splashing, a slapstick ballet,
Where mermaids giggle at the end of the bay.
The horizon bows low, with colors that tease,
And seagulls take jibes at the children's knees.

So raise a glass to this ocean parade,
Where laughter and cheer are never delayed.
With every splash, we embrace the delight,
In this watery world, everything's just right!

Lullabies of the Coral Reef

Coral colonies sing in a bustling choir,
While sea cucumbers twirl in a dance of desire.
The starry-eyed fish, all dressed up so fine,
Join in the night, our oceanic line.

Giant clams clap like they've won a grand prize,
With oysters giggling, they shield their surprise.
In this riot of color, both vivid and bright,
The reef holds secrets in the heart of the night.

A pufferfish blushes, puffing up tall,
While clownfish chuckle, it's a comedic ball.
The octopus chuckles, painting the scene,
With playful gestures, oh what a machine!

So close your eyes, let the currents take sway,
Drift on the laughter, let your worries decay.
In the lullabies sung from the depths, you'll see,
The ocean shimmers with jests wild and free.

Fluid Dance of the Ocean's Breath

The sea does a jig, waves round and spry,
Seagulls start laughing, oh my, oh my!
Turtles in sandals slide to the beat,
Crabs doing cha-chas with clammy feet.

Salt shakers are dancing, what a delight,
As fish flip and splash, what a curious sight!
Jellyfish giggle and float with such grace,
While octopuses juggle, oh what a race!

A starfish in shades lounges on the shore,
With a drink in its hand, it shouts, "More, more!"
The sun's playing DJ, cranking the tunes,
While the beach ball plays tag with the dunes.

What a hoot this ocean can be, oh dear!
With shells acting silly, it's parties we cheer.
Let's sway to the rhythm, join in the spree,
As the breeze tells our secrets, just you and me.

Caresses of a Sunlit Afternoon

Sunbeams are tickling the sandy shore,
While loungers in hats ask for just one more.
Ice cream cones wobble, melting so fast,
As kids take a plunge and splash with a blast.

Chairs are upchucking from too much fun,
While flip-flops take off, on their own run!
The laughter of seagulls, a comical choir,
As sunscreen mishaps become our desire.

Coconuts chuckle with drinks held so neat,
As cheers from the beach volleyball meet.
Breeze carries giggles, a joyous parade,
With umbrellas doing the dance they've made.

Sunset bursts forth with a wink and a grin,
As shadows take over, let this joke begin.
Just like a crab in its sideways frolic,
The laughter we share is absolutely iconic.

Driftwood Dreams on Serene Waters

A log's on a journey, just floating along,
With a barnacle chorus singing its song.
Waves play hopscotch on a driftwood stage,
With fish in the front row, all set to engage.

Splash of a belly flop, oh what a sight,
As seaweed wigs dance in the glowing light.
The splash from the dock brings laughter unfurled,
While crustaceans calculate how to twirl.

A clam gives a wink, can you believe?
While plankton dance small, never deceived.
As mermaids join in with flips and with flair,
Who knew the ocean had such a dare?

With driftwood debates on the best kind of fish,
They sip salty coffee and share their wish.
On this watery floor, the hilarity swells,
In dreams off the coast, where muttering tells.

Soft Voices of Faraway Isles

Waves whisper secrets that tickle the sand,
While clams tell jokes—who knew they were grand?
The coconut palms are doubling over,
As the seashells exchange their fine jewelry cover.

A pelican flaps, and hope in its eyes,
As crabs wear their hats, a comical prize.
Fish flip their tails, a dazzling display,
Catching the sunlight in a sparkling ballet.

With breezes that nudge, oh what a delight,
A picnic on shore becomes quite the sight.
Sandcastles giggle as they stand tall and proud,
While beach towels unfurl, oh they're really loud!

A slapstick of fun beneath the sunbeam,
As children chase waves, it's a family dream.
So come join the laughter, don't miss out on play,
With tides full of mischief, let's splash, come what may!

Celestial Echoes of Ocean's Heart

The seagulls squawk in a giddy dance,
Chasing each other, they prance with a chance.
A crab in a tux, with a top hat so neat,
Stomps with his claws, oh, what a treat!

The waves laugh out, bobbing like a child,
With bubbles that burst, all frothy and wild.
Starfish shoot jokes from their sandy abode,
While turtles roll in the chilly mode!

A mermaid sings tunes, in an off-key style,
With dolphins that giggle, and swim for a while.
They all join the party beneath the moon's glow,
As crickets play maracas, stealing the show!

So grab a drink, let the ocean outshine,
Join in the fun, where it's always divine.
For in this realm of sand, salt, and dance,
Life's a hilarious swing, not left to chance!

Heartbeats of Nature's Serenade

A parrot babbles in colors so bright,
Telling old tales with all of its might.
Frogs play trumpets, they're ready to boast,
While fireflies waltz, oh, so lovely, a host!

The trees sway rhythmically, side to side,
With raccoons in tuxedos, they laugh, not hide.
Squirrels hold acorns like trophies of pride,
As nature itself puts on a wild ride!

Breezes carry gossip from leaf to tall tree,
As ants host parties, so literally.
The moon giggles down, in a silver-lit room,
While the night holds secrets and endless zoom!

So take a moment, join the giggling spree,
For in this wild life, there's joy, can't you see?
Nature's a show, where comedy streams,
And laughter's the thread that binds all our dreams!

Beneath the Stars of a Midnight Shore

Beneath the stars, the crabs hold a feast,
While jellyfish dance like they're lost in a beast.
The moon chuckles bright, in a silvery laugh,
As starfish play poker, oh what a gaff!

Sandcastles squabble with shells in the night,
While seahorses race in a whirlwind of light.
A clam sings a tune, to the beats of the tide,
As everyone joins in for the midnight ride!

The wind tells stories with a cheeky swoon,
As fish flash their scales, all under the moon.
A pelican flaps, wearing mismatched socks,
While everyone giggles, and time gently clocks.

So dance on the shore, let the silliness reign,
For laughter's the treasure, in joy and in strain.
At this midnight bash, where the sea comes alive,
We'll celebrate fun, and together we thrive!

Tales on a Cinnamon Breeze

On a breeze so sweet, like cinnamon delight,
The iguanas gossip under the light.
Coconuts grin with a cheeky flair,
As palm trees chuckle, swaying in the air!

A parrot tells tales in a playful tone,
As crabs in the corner discuss their best bone.
The sun is a jester, with rays all around,
Turning beach games into a laughter-bound.

The sand is a pillow where dreams come to play,
While flip-flops flutter in a tangy ballet.
Seashells gossip about fishy affairs,
While the breeze carries secrets and silly lairs!

Raise your drinks high, let the fun never cease,
For the beach is a canvas of joy and peace.
With laughter like bubbles rising ever free,
We'll dance on this breeze, enjoying the spree!

Breezy Notes in Twilight's Glow

A parrot in the palm tree sings,
Forgetful of its colorings.
It cracks a joke, it tells a tale,
While seagulls giggle, some turn pale.

In the evening's amber light,
Sandcastles run from seashell fright.
They tumble down, it's quite the show,
The tide laughs hard, won't let them grow.

A crab dons shades, stylish and bright,
Dancing sideways, oh what a sight!
The sun winks down, it's time to tease,
As ocean waves start to sneeze.

Yes, a breeze brings a vibrant dance,
Where every critter takes a chance.
So let the laughter fill the air,
For twilight's glow is quite the affair.

Shadows Cast by Whispering Winds

A shadow bathed in golden hue,
Steals a snack, once meant for two.
The coconut laughs, it rolls away,
While giggling waves begin to play.

A lizard struts, its tail so bright,
Tripping over, oh what a sight!
The toads all cheer, they croak out loud,
While palm trees sway, oh they're so proud.

With every gust, a tale unfolds,
A fish wearing sunglasses, so bold.
The wind carries cackles, wild and free,
As laughter echoes, quite cheekily.

So let the breezes crack a smile,
In shadows that dance, mile after mile.
Where every critter joins the jest,
And life on the shore is truly blessed.

Finding Solitude in Ocean's Sigh

A crab in a hammock sways with glee,
While jellyfish float, sipping iced tea.
They ponder life, what could it bring?
With barnacles laughing at the fling.

Seagulls dive, putting on a show,
One wigs out, yells "Hey, let's go!"
Waves wager bets, all in good fun,
As the sun hurries down, it must run.

A hermit crab starts a dance routine,
In a conch shell, feeling quite keen.
With each little twirl and wild slide,
Crabs and fish cheer, they're filled with pride.

Amidst the chaos, a calm prevails,
As laughter rides the ocean's trails.
For finding peace in every sigh,
Is the trick, oh my, oh my!

Secrets of the Clifftop's Song

Atop the cliffs, the gulls take bets,
On who can dive without regrets.
With flapping wings and friendly squawks,
They play like children, in heartfelt talks.

The wind spins tales, a jester's game,
Of dolphins dancing, all the same.
A tuna pops up, flips in delight,
While crabs go clam digging, out of sight.

On the edge of thrills, the rocks all giggle,
As waves come crashing, they dance and wiggle.
Secrets wrapped in salty air,
Tickle the senses, everywhere.

So listen close to what's around,
For laughter and joy in nature abound.
With every note in the sea's embrace,
Life's a funny, wild, sweet race.

Memoirs of a Salt-Kissed Sky

Seagulls squawk like they own the place,
Trying to steal my lunch, oh what a chase!
Salty air tickles my nose and toes,
I swear that I saw a crab in a pose!

Flip-flops flapping, a dance on the shore,
I tripped on my towel, fell flat—oh, the roar!
The sun's hot embrace, a tan that's too bright,
I'm now a lobster, it's quite the sight!

Shells tell stories of treasures unknown,
Yet here I am, just seeking my phone.
Breezes tease hair, like a bad shampoo,
Why didn't I pack a cap? Who knew?

With each splash, laughter echoes and swells,
A mermaid giggles, oh the tales she tells!
Salt-kissed skin, I dance with the breeze,
Life's a beach, so let's laugh with ease!

A Quiet Dance in the Glistening Sand

Sands on my toes, like tickles from fate,
I bust a move, though my friends just await.
Crabs join in, those pinchers in style,
I'm leading this dance, with a wiggle and smile!

The sun starts to dip, I'm lost in a trance,
A seagull scoffs as I wiggle and prance.
"Who taught you those moves?" the tide seems to tease,
I just shrug and laugh, it's all meant to please!

A starfish lounges with rays on its back,
I join in the sun, my moves never lack.
"Eh-eh! This groove is for toes in the sand!"
But the tide rolls in - oh, where's my cool stand?

As dusk settles down, the moon starts to glow,
My friends all join in, with a shimmy and flow.
Glistening sands are our floor for the night,
Complete with a crab who forgot his plight!

Lighthouses of the Heart

Beacons glow bright on a darkened shore,
A lighthouse keeper who loves to explore.
But oh, what a sight, when he barrels around,
Tripping on rocks, he falls to the ground!

With every wave crashing, his lantern sways,
He dances with shadows in odd little ways.
He tells tales of ships lost, but wait, what's that?
A seaweed monster? No, just his old hat!

The light spins with laughter, like hopes intertwined,
As mermaids below laugh, oh they're so kind!
"Is that all you got?" they giggle and tease,
He smiles back, saying, "Let's all catch the breeze!"

Each flicker's a wink, a smile from the heart,
Guiding lost sailors, who don't know their part.
So here's to the keeper, his quirks and his light,
In the boisterous dance of the waves in flight!

Nature's Calls in Swaying Coconuts

Coconuts giggle in the swaying trees,
They whisper sweet secrets to floating bees.
"Watch out below!" yells the palm's leafy crown,
While I dodge falling fruit and tumble down!

A parrot lands next, flamboyant and loud,
"Who needs a vacation when you're this proud?"
With colors so bright, it starts a grand jam,
Cracking up crabs as they win like a champ!

The breeze brings a tune, a song full of cheer,
"Dance with us now, you've nothing to fear!"
I sway with the palms, like a feathery fool,
It seems I've joined in on nature's own school!

So here on the island, under the sky,
I laugh with the critters as time passes by.
Let's raise a coconut and toast to the feast,
Life's silly and sweet, let's dance like a beast!

Echoes of the Tempest's Nurture

The seagull steals my sandwich fast,
As I sip tea, the breezes blast.
A crab in shorts, he plays it cool,
Dances round like a wacky fool.

The waves clap hands, a silly cheer,
While dolphins grin and swim near here.
Footprints in sand, a message sent,
"Bring snacks!" is what the ocean meant.

A fisherman sings, a comical tune,
While slippery fish all plan a swoon.
Each cast and reel, a laugh or two,
Nature's comedy, what a view!

Yet here I sit with grains in hair,
The beachball bounces, unaware.
Oh island joys, you're full of fun,
Where breezes play, and laughter's spun.

Serenading the Moonlit Waters

The moon makes faces, oh so bright,
While waves engage in a splashy fight.
Fiddler crabs with their tiny fiddles,
Play tunes so off-key, they bring giggles.

A starfish lounging, strikes a pose,
While a sea turtle trips on his toes.
The boats swing low, a laugh parade,
With mermaids grinning, the show's well laid!

Night's chilly breeze is full of glee,
As I chase shadows, they flee from me.
Oh lighthouse beams that wink and tease,
Guide me home through the night's cool breeze.

Each wave that crashes, a joke it spills,
In laughter's wave, oh how time thrills.
Where sea and sky become a jest,
In moonlit waters, I find my rest.

A Lifting Whisper of the Tide

The tide rolls in, a slippery friend,
It tickles toes, around it bends.
A mermaid calls with a dolphin's cheer,
While starfish giggle at all we fear.

The sandcastle kings throw a grand ball,
With tidecasters dancing, they have a ball.
A sand crab DJ spins a track,
As shells join in, there's no turning back.

Oh, why'd the oyster cross the sand?
To meet a clam with the finest band!
Their voices rise, a comical tune,
As pelicans laugh at the light of the moon.

"Watch out!" I shout, as a wave comes near,
It splashes my towel, oh dear, oh dear!
Yet laughter rings out, it's all a breeze,
For every trifle, I'm still here with ease.

Melodies in Stillness After the Storm

Post-storm sighs, the skies so clear,
While seagulls jive, spreading good cheer.
A turtle hums a jazzy beat,
And crabs two-step on sandy feet.

The palm trees sway in a breezy dance,
While coconuts roll, oh what a chance!
Each breeze a note in nature's song,
A chorus of laughter, where we belong.

Oh, the shells have tales, and they know
Of underwater parties, secrets below.
They whisper jokes to the waves at play,
While sunbeams giggle, brightening the day.

Stillness reigns, but it's a prank,
As a wave tiptoes, with stealthy flank.
"Splash!" it cries, and we all flee,
Yet in this mirth, we're wild and free!

Echoes of Love Across the Water

In a boat that's leaking, oh what a sight,
Two lovers are paddling with all their might.
They sing a sweet tune while splashing around,
But the fish join in, how they leap and bound!

They toss in some bread, it flies like a dart,
The gulls start to squawk, it's quite the art.
One fell in the drink, oh what a mess,
These echoes of love are quite the jest!

With the breeze as their guide, hiccups of cheer,
They sail past a sign that reads, "No Beer Here!"
But laughter erupts like waves at their feet,
Two hearts made of giggles, life's funny treat.

As the sun starts to set, they row to the shore,
The sand tickles toes, they always want more.
With pockets of seashells, they trip on their bliss,
This watery love is sealed with a kiss.

Resounding Hush of the Coral Bay

In the calm of the bay, a clam took a nap,
While crabs danced around in a silly trap.
A parrot squawks loudly, claims he's the champ,
But the shrimp are just giggling, forming a stamp!

The surf laughs too hard, it dries all the tears,
As seaweed does jiggles, ballet of peers.
A boat drifts on by, with pirates so bold,
But they're all here for treasure—old socks and mold!

An octopus grins, he's quite the charmer,
With eight arms in motion, you might just disarm her.
But all that she caught was a crab in a whirl,
Who slipped on the foam, now is dancing a twirl!

Meanwhile in the quiet, the sun takes a bow,
As jellyfish tumble, with grace, oh wow!
So here's to the bay, a chorus of jest,
Where laughter and seaweed are truly the best!

Serenades from the Edge of the Sea

A snail with a banjo is strumming a tune,
While seagulls are grooving 'neath light of the moon.
The waves tap their toes, in rhythm divine,
They join in the fun, making seashells align.

In the splash of a wave, a fish sings in glee,
He's got quite the voice for a creature so free.
The crabs bring the beat, they're snappy and quick,
With shells for a drum, it's a nautical trick!

The breeze takes a bow, and messes my hair,
As dolphins pop up with a flip and a flair.
They join in the song, do you hear that refrain?
A chorus of laughter, all wedged in the main.

As the stars blink above, a lobster's the star,
He's waltzing on rocks, oh how bizarre!
With a crabby backup, it's quite the affair,
This serenade's silly, but we just don't care!

Colors of the Breezy Sunrise

Oh look at the colors that dance in the sky,
Like jellybeans spilled, as the seagulls all fly.
A parakeet paints from his perch on a tree,
While surfers do flips, saltwater, oh me!

The sand becomes golden, a soft toasty hug,
As starfish perform on the soft, sandy rug.
The sunrise is giggling, can't hold back its glee,
While crabs crack up at a red anemone.

With a splash and a leap, the fish join the show,
All colors collide, oh where did they go?
Holding laughter like shells, the beach starts to wake,
As morning unfolds, it's a colorful quake!

Come join the fun where the sun loves to tease,
A laughing horizon, the colors appease.
With each tickling ray, a promise of cheer,
We'll dance through the day with smiles, oh dear!

Breezes Carrying Forgotten Stories

The sandy shores chuckle with glee,
As sea turtles dance, you just can't see.
A crab in a tux, so dapper and neat,
Holds court with the waves, a fanciful feat.

A pelican swoops, quite sure of his aim,
Dropping fish snacks, oh what a game!
The gulls all scream, with laughter so loud,
As beach umbrellas take flight, so proud.

Laughter echoes through the sunset glow,
A coconut falls, putting on a show.
Where flip-flops are lost and sunburns abound,
The breeze tells tales of mischief profound.

By the firelight, tales take to the skies,
Of mermaids who tripped 'cause they wore clumsy ties.
While starfish giggle at the moon's silly grin,
Every sandy footstep, ready to begin.

Embrace of the Evocative Wind

The wind wraps around like a snug little hug,
Tickling all noses, just giving a shrug.
It's a joyful ruckus, each leaf starts to play,
As kites kite-fly in a hilarious fray.

A beach ball bumps and jumpily rolls,
While seagulls trade winks and jokes with the shoals.
The sand's got rhythm, it jiggles and sways,
As the breeze giggles on these sunny days.

Swaying palm trees join in the fun,
With a twist and a turn, they're never outdone.
A coconut sitcom unfolds on the shore,
With fruits sharing laughs, they just can't ignore.

When twilight arrives, they share secret laughs,
Under the stars, they'll recount their gaffes.
A gentle reminder, life's too short to frown,
Embrace the giggles, feel the joy all around.

Veils of the Soft-Hearted Tide

The waves tiptoe in, all gentle and shy,
With a splash and a giggle, they float on by.
Little fish peek out, like kids playing hide,
While starfish remark, "Let's go for a ride!"

The tide rolls in with a humorous spin,
Tickling toes, where the fun does begin.
A buoy's got style, bobbing with flair,
A jester at sea, playing without a care.

Oh, the floaties parade in a grand silly race,
Where seaweed wiggles like it's got a sweet face.
And clams crack up at the jokes of the crabs,
In the soft-hearted tide, there are no drab jabs.

As night falls, the waves whisper a tune,
Of sandcastles wrecked by the light of the moon.
With giggling gulls singing all through the night,
The tide rolls with laughter, oh what a sight!

The Lull of Distant Horizons

The sunset stretches, painting skies bold,
With oranges and pinks that never grow old.
Sailing ships are laughing, oh what a sight,
As they tip their hats to the stars that bite.

A hammock swings low, creaking with cheer,
While sleepyheads snore, dreaming of beer.
Breezes tease lightly, they poke and they prod,
Making days drift on, like an endless façade.

The horizon giggles, a mischievous tease,
As ships ride the waves, caught up in the breeze.
A dolphin jumps high, in playful delight,
Playing tag with the sun, until it's goodnight.

When it's time to rest, the stars come out bright,
With whispers of moonbeams that shimmer and bite.
The lull of the day, sleepy and sweet,
Ends the fun jaunt of this oceanic retreat.

Voices Carried on the Distant Surf

In the tide, a seagull squawks,
"Dive for snacks, forget the clocks!"
Crabs on patrol, with sideways step,
Stealing fries, not a care or prep.

The surf so loud, yet still they giggle,
Making waves, like a dance, a wiggle.
Fish with shades swim by with flair,
Chasing bait like it's a dare.

Sandcastles rise, but then they fall,
As kids run past, one gives a squall.
The ocean laughs, it's a merry tune,
With dolphins darting beneath the moon.

Tides retreat — a game of tag,
While jellyfish just laugh and wag.
Each splash a jest, each foam a cheer,
In the salty air, we persevere!

Dreams Unfurled in the Sea Breeze

A kite soars high, on a laughter thread,
Its tail a noodle, joy widespread.
Children cheer, as it starts to dip,
"Hey! Hand me that, it's on a trip!"

Seagulls gossip about the fun,
With tales of fish and how to run.
Each shout a spark, each smile a star,
Living dreams, wherever we are.

Sandy toes dance on the shore,
Shuffling to tunes they can't ignore.
Each wave a giggle, each breeze a tease,
Nature's playground, full of ease.

When night descends, the fun won't cease,
For the moon's a lantern, offering peace.
Laughter lingers in the salty air,
As dreams unfurl, without a care!

Threads of Serenity in the Changing Tides

Sand hats bob, a majestic sight,
As footprints vanish with delight.
Shells whisper tales of ocean lore,
Keeping secrets from the shore.

Shimmers dance on each gentle wave,
While crabs race, oh, how they brave!
Each tide a jest, each current a laugh,
Nature's own crazy photograph.

The sun winks down, "Let's have some fun!"
Beach balls bounce, while ice cream's on the run.
Gulls overhead, screeching in glee,
As if they're singing just for me.

A breeze that tickles, a breeze that sighs,
As friends gather 'neath cerulean skies.
With sandy toes and sun-kissed pride,
In this lively world, we all abide.

Caressing Whims of the Evening Air

The sunset paints a canvas bright,
As children chase fireflies with delight.
Giggling echoes, like music, rise,
With twinkling stars to claim the skies.

The breeze brings whispers of playful schemes,
While parents sip their iced cold dreams.
Laughter follows, a game of catch,
As ice cream drips, oh, what a match!

Lawn chairs sway, stories drift along,
With tales of conches and a seagull's song.
The night hums soft, with its cool embrace,
In a world of fun, where smiles find grace.

With every laugh, the moments grow,
In the gentle pull of the evening's flow.
Here's to the memories we've spun like threads,
In this cozy nook, where joy spreads!

www.ingramcontent.com/pod-product-compliance
Lightning Source LLC
Chambersburg PA
CBHW072130070526
44585CB00016B/1611